This journal belongs to: ....

Phone number: ....

Email address: ....

Other contact numbers: ....

....

....

....

THE

ALMANAC

JOURNAL

LIA LEENDERTZ

With illustrations by Rachel Grant

MITCHELL BEAZLEY

An Hachette UK Company
www.hachette.co.uk

First published in Great Britain in 2020 by Mitchell Beazley,
an imprint of Octopus Publishing Group Ltd
Carmelite House
50 Victoria Embankment
London EC4Y 0DZ
www.octopusbooks.co.uk

ISBN 978-1-78472-643-0

A CIP catalogue record for this book is available from the British Library.

Printed and bound in China

10 9 8 7 6 5 4 3 2 1

Publishing Director: Stephanie Jackson
Creative Director: Jonathan Christie
Designer: Matt Cox at Newman+Eastwood
Editor: Ella Parsons
Copy Editor: Alison Wormleighton
Assistant Production Controller: Serena Savini

Acknowledgements

Thanks to everyone who has worked on making this journal such a lovely
thing. To Rachel Grant for the glorious illustrations that bring it alive, and
designer Matt Cox for shepherding all of my ideas into a calm and beautiful
whole. Thanks to everyone at Octopus: Stephanie Jackson for overseeing and
cheerleading, Ella Parsons for calm and considered editing, Jonathan Christie
for excellent art direction, as well as Alison Wormleighton and Jane Birch for
careful copyediting and proofreading. Thank you also to my agent Adrian
Sington for championing the idea.

CONTENTS

INTRODUCTION

Welcome to the *Almanac Journal*, a place for you to create
your own personal almanac, starting and ending at any point
in the year that suits you. An almanac is a book about a year,
and you might know my own annual seasonal almanacs, which
cover the sky at night, tides, gardening, nature, food, rituals
and more. Readers kept asking me if I could leave a few pages
blank here and there for their own notes, and I realised that
– as much as they enjoyed reading my almanacs – there was a
strong desire among them to create their own. That is what this
journal is for.

This is your space to write down all of the things you notice
about the year's turning, and your own reactions to it. It is
based roughly on the subjects that fill my own almanacs. There
are pages where you can note all of the firsts (first swift, first
rose, first frost); space for weather and tide observations; night-
sky spotting pages; a place to squirrel away your secret foraging
locations – and to jot down the recipes you use to cook your
finds. Here you can map your garden through the year, and
keep records of what you do in it and your plans for the future.
You can think about the rituals that you like to play out during
each season, and record your thoughts and reflections as one
season runs into the next.

There are also pages for pressed flowers, pressed seaweed,
sketches and pictures. My great hope is that the *Almanac
Journal* ends up messy and stuffed with bits and bobs, some
pages warped from being out in the drizzle, bits of sand stuck
in their gutters, ends of feathers and crisp leaves poking out
when the journal is (never quite) closed. I hope, too, that it
will be a tool for helping you to pause and take notice of the
changing seasons and what they mean to you. This is your
almanac, about your year. Please make it your own.

Lia Leendertz

FIRSTS AND LASTS

Keep track of the small but significant markers of the year by jotting down some firsts and – where you notice them – lasts. In some cases there may not be a definite 'last', but you can still use this space to map the length of, say, bluebell season this year, or the length of time your neighbour's beautiful roses are in bloom. You might want to compare these dates next year, or just use this as an aid to looking and noticing, and measuring the year's passing.

Primrose

First: .... Last: ....

Notes: ....

....

Frogspawn

First: .... Last: ....

Notes: ....

....

Magnolia

First: .... Last: ....

Notes: ....

....

Asparagus

First: .... Last: ....

Notes: ....

....

Butterfly

First: .... Last: ....

Notes: ....

....

Bumblebee

First: .... Last: ....

Notes: ....

....

Dandelion flower

First: .... Last: ....

Notes: ....

....

Strawberry

First: .... Last: ....

Notes: ....

....

Bluebell

First: .... Last: ....

Notes: ....

....

Gambolling lamb

First: .... Last: ....

Notes: ....

....

Rose

First: .... Last: ....

Notes: ....

....

Swift

First: .... Last: ....

Notes: ....

....

Swallow

First: .... Last: ....

Notes: ....

....

Picnic

First: .... Last: ....

Notes: ....

....

Barbecue

First: .... Last: ....

Notes: ....

....

Autumn leaf falling

First: .... Last: ....

Notes: ....

....

Dewy spider's web

First: .... Last: ....

Notes: ....

....

Pavement conker

First: .... Last: ....

Notes: ....

....

Wild mushroom

First: .... Last: ....

Notes: ....

....

Robin

First: .... Last: ....

Notes: ....

....

Frozen puddle

First: .... Last: ....

Notes: ....

....

WEATHER

WEATHER LOG

Keep track of weekly maximum and minimum temperatures, rain volume, highest wind speeds and wind direction. You will need a few basic instruments (see the list opposite).

	Max temp	Min temp	Rain volume
Week 1			
Week 2			
Week 3			
Week 4			
Week 5			
Week 6			
Week 7			
Week 8			
Week 9			
Week 10			
Week 11			
Week 12			
Week 13			
Week 14			

Basic weather-monitoring instruments

- A 'max–min' thermometer, which will record the highest and lowest temperatures over a given period
- A rain gauge
- An anemometer (wind gauge) and weather vane to record wind speed and direction

Or combine the lot by buying an electronic wireless weather station to place outdoors – it will relay weather data back to your comfy armchair.

Max wind speed	Wind direction	General trend

	Max temp	Min temp	Rain volume
Week 15			
Week 16			
Week 17			
Week 18			
Week 19			
Week 20			
Week 21			
Week 22			
Week 23			
Week 24			
Week 25			
Week 26			
Week 27			
Week 28			
Week 29			
Week 30			
Week 31			
Week 32			
Week 33			

Max wind speed   Wind direction   General trend

	Max temp	Min temp	Rain volume
Week 34			
Week 35			
Week 36			
Week 37			
Week 38			
Week 39			
Week 40			
Week 41			
Week 42			
Week 43			
Week 44			
Week 45			
Week 46			
Week 47			
Week 48			
Week 49			
Week 50			
Week 51			
Week 52			

Max wind speed	Wind direction	General trend

CLOUDS, WEATHER PHENOMENA AND RAINBOWS

Look up, and make a note of any meteorological beauties that you see.

Date:

☐ **Cumulonimbus clouds**
These tall and threatening clouds mass on the horizon, dazzlingly white and densely fluffy like over-whipped cream, but revealing dark grey and black insides. They are said to indicate that a storm is coming.

☐ **Rainbow**
A rainbow is formed when the sun shines through rain droplets, which refract and reflect it into the full spectrum of colours.

☐ **Cumulus clouds**
The little white fluffy clouds, floating in a blue sky, are cumulus clouds.

☐ **Crepuscular rays**
These beautiful shafts of light, piercing clouds, most often appear around sunrise and sunset.

☐ **Cirrocumulus clouds, or mackerel sky**
This high-altitude layer of cloudlets can indicate that a change in the weather is coming.

☐ **Halo**
Sun and moon halos are circular rainbows or white rings caused by ice crystals in the earth's atmosphere refracting and reflecting the light as it passes through the crystals.

WEATHER EVENTS

Major storms   Date: ....   Notes: ....

....

....

High winds   Date: ....   Notes: ....

....

....

Snow   Date: ....   Notes: ....

....

....

Hail   Date: ....   Notes: ....

....

....

Fog   Date: ....   Notes: ....

....

....

Dew   Date: ....   Notes: ....

....

....

Flooding   Date: ....   Notes: ....
....
....

Heatwave   Date: ....   Notes: ....
....
....

Hottest day   Date: ....   Notes: ....
....
....

Coldest day   Date: ....   Notes: ....
....
....

Last frost   Date: ....   Notes: ....
....
....

First frost   Date: ....   Notes: ....
....
....

GENERAL WEATHER PATTERNS

At the end of each month, look back on your records and sum up the general weather patterns of the past month. This will allow you to confidently say, 'Wasn't that a dry July?' and so on, which will impress people. It will also be useful to look back on at the same time next year.

January

....

....

....

February

....

....

....

March

....

....

....

April

....

....

....

May

....

....

....

June

July

August

September

October

November

December

THE SEA

TIDES

Use the space on these pages to map out the tides for the times you are near the beach. While you must, of course, use a tide timetable if accuracy is necessary for safety, it is actually quite easy to roughly calculate tides yourself. Make a note of high and low tide times on your first day by the beach – you could ask a local, look at an RNLI lifesavers' information board or check a tide timetable for this. The following day's tides will be roughly half an hour later, the day after that will be half an hour later again, and so on. Use this to plan your week's beach activities.

Spring tides: Is there a spring tide while you are at the beach? A spring tide occurs a day or two after a full or new moon, and it is more extreme – with higher highs and lower lows. A low spring tide is the perfect time to go rock-pooling, fossil-hunting or mudlarking. Calculate yours here by finding out the date of the full or new moon and adding a couple of days.

Week commencing

	High tide		Low tide	
	am	pm	am	pm
Day 1				
Day 2				
Day 3				
Day 4				
Day 5				
Day 6				
Day 7				

Date of full or new moon:

Likely date of spring tide:

Week commencing

....

	High tide		Low tide	
	am	pm	am	pm
Day 1				
Day 2				
Day 3				
Day 4				
Day 5				
Day 6				
Day 7				

Date of full or new moon: ....

Likely date of spring tide: ....

Week commencing

....

	High tide		Low tide	
	am	pm	am	pm
Day 1				
Day 2				
Day 3				
Day 4				
Day 5				
Day 6				
Day 7				

Date of full or new moon: ....

Likely date of spring tide: ....

SPOTTER'S GUIDE – SEASIDE

Look out for these things at the seaside, and when you find them, tick them off and make notes.

Jellyfish
You can sometimes spot them in the water below you when looking off of a pier or harbour, or you may find a less lucky one washed up on the sand.

Date: Notes:

Mermaid's purse
You may come across a mermaid's purse tangled up in seaweed at the tideline, and although it looks like seaweed, this is actually the egg case of the lesser spotted dogfish. Some sharks and rays have similar egg cases.

Date: Notes:

By-the-wind sailor
A rare find. By-the-wind sailors spend most of their lives many miles from shore, using their sail-like appendages to travel across the ocean. You may find them washed up on southern and western beaches, particularly after a westerly gale.

Date: Notes:

Thrift
Also known as sea pink. The pretty, rounded pink heads of flowers sprout from tiny nooks in cliffs during the summer.

Date: Notes:

☐ **Grey seals**
Winter is the best time to spot grey seals as they come out to calve on remote beaches.

Date: .... Notes: ....

....

....

☐ **Shore crab**
One of the most common crabs. Look for it in rock pools.

Date: .... Notes: ....

....

....

☐ **Limpets**
See limpets stuck fast to the sides of rocks that have been submerged.

Date: .... Notes: ....

....

....

☐ **Sea anemone**
Look for it in rock pools. If you touch a sea anemone with your finger, it will try to catch you.

Date: .... Notes: ....

....

....

HOW TO PRESS SEAWEED AND FLOWERS

Pressing seaweed, flowers and leaves turns them from living and breathing (and soon wilting and rotting) things into timeless pieces of art. It is simple to do and you can stick the dried seaweed, flowers and leaves into this journal or even frame them and hang them on the wall.

To press seaweed
You will need:
• Shallow tray
• Salt water or fresh water
• Thick paper, such as watercolour or cartridge paper
• Scissors
• Pencil
• Tweezers
• Newspaper
• Kitchen roll
• Heavy books

1 Select a piece of seaweed and put it in the tray with a little water.
2 Cut a piece of paper to fit, and write the name of the seaweed (if known) and the date and location of collection on one corner of the paper. Slip it into the tray underneath the seaweed.
3 Tip the tray so that the seaweed is only shallowly covered, and use your fingers or tweezers to spread out the fronds.
4 Keeping the tray tipped and the fronds spread, slide the paper very slowly and carefully up and out of the water. Allow excess water to drip off and then place the paper on a wodge of newspaper.
5 Cover the seaweed with a piece of kitchen roll and then top with more newpaper and a pile of heavy books.
6 Change the kitchen paper and newspaper daily for a few days, after which the paper and seaweed should be dry and pressed and the seaweed naturally stuck to the paper.

To press flowers and leaves
Press flowers and leaves in exactly the same way as above, but without the tray of water and the need to change the papers. Arrange your flowers on a piece of paper, cover with a piece of kitchen roll and then newspaper, and press with a pile of books for several days.

BEACH FINDS

Stick beach finds and pressed seaweed and flowers here, and perhaps even use a little smear of glue to keep a scattering of sand in place. Alternatively, you could use this space for beach sketches or photos.

THE SKY AT NIGHT

HOW TO SKY-WATCH

Find your darkest sky: While we can't all aspire to the giddy depths of an Exmoor or Highlands dark sky, there are a few things we can do to make the most of our position in order to see as much as we can. In built-up areas there will generally be too much light pollution to see a great deal, with the (very excellent) exceptions of the bright planets and the moon. If you can get out into the countryside, away from towns and cities, you will see so much more. If that isn't possible, you can still make the most of city and town sky-watching. Site yourself facing towards a large, unlit area (a park, the sea, an allotment site) and then make sure you have no lights shining directly into your eyes – position yourself in shadow. Take your time and let your eyes adjust, and you will see far more than if you just walked along the street and looked up.

Use a star chart or star app: On pages 48–55 you will find some star charts. Select the one for the correct time of year, find one of the easily picked-out constellations or asterisms (clusters of stars within constellations) – the Plough and Orion are always good places to start – and from there work your way out to other constellations. If you are still struggling you could use a star-finding app such as Star Walk; you point your smartphone at the sky and the app tells you what you're looking at.

Use binoculars or a telescope: You don't need either of these to watch the sky but, once you have picked out a few basic constellations, there is a lot of fun to be had in looking a little closer at the spaces in between: clusters, galaxies and nebulas will hove magically into view. Binoculars and telescopes are also wonderful for taking a closer look at the planets, and to appreciate the full pockmarked and cratered glory of the moon.

Get comfy and warm: Winter is a great time to watch the sky, as it gets dark so early, plus cooler air is clearer and less hazy than warm air. But, of course, winter sky-watching means getting chilly. Find a place to sit – a deckchair will put you at just the right angle – swathe yourself in blankets, have a Thermos to hand, and watch the show. Spring and autumn are also good sky-watching times, but in summer you will have to stay up late in order to see all but the brightest stars.

NIGHT-SKY PHENOMENA

Keep a look out for satellites, meteors and other phenomena of the night sky.

International Space Station pass
The International Space Station makes 15.7 orbits of the earth every day. You can see it very clearly if it passes over at dawn or dusk, when it reflects the sun but the sky is still dark. It is always manned, and it is wonderful to look up and think of the strange lives of the astronauts within. It always travels in a roughly west-to-east direction but may be high in the sky or low to the horizon. Use an app such as I.S.S. Tracker to find when it is passing over.

Date: .... Time: ....

Your location: ....

Notes: ....

....

Date: .... Time: ....

Your location: ....

Notes: ....

....

Date: .... Time: ....

Your location: ....

Notes: ....

....

Iridium flares

These are caused by satellites tilting and catching the sun, sending a brief and very bright beam down towards earth. They look like slowly moving stars that brighten and then quickly fade. They are visible only for moments, but certainly long enough to impress when you airily wave a hand and pronounce that there will be a flash in the sky in about two minutes. You will need to use a tracker app such as Heavens-Above.

Date: Time:

Your location:

Notes:

Date: Time:

Your location:

Notes:

The Milky Way

You need a good dark sky in order to see the Milky Way, which is, in fact, a glimpse out towards the edge of our disc-shaped galaxy, which is so thick with distant stars that it turns a band of the sky a paler shade.

Date: Time:

Your location:

Notes:

Date: Time:

Your location:

Notes:

The aurora borealis or northern lights

The aurora borealis appears when the earth's magnetosphere (the area around the earth controlled by its magnetic force) is disturbed by solar winds, resulting in a magnificent and colourful display that sweeps across the sky. Sightings in the British Isles tend only to be in the far north, but occasionally good shows are visible farther south.

Date: .... Time: ....

Your location: ....

Notes: ....

....

Date: .... Time: ....

Your location: ....

Notes: ....

....

Meteor shower

This is caused by the earth ploughing through the dust left behind by comets, and that dust burning up on contact with our atmosphere, creating meteorites, or shooting stars. There are a number of notable and reliable meteor showers through the year. Use a resource such as *The Almanac* to find out the best dates for spotting.

Date: .... Time: ....

Your location: ....

Notes: ....

....

Date: .... Time: ....

Your location: ....

Notes: ....

....

THE MOON

The moon is our most visible and immediate reminder that the cosmos lies just outside our windows. Look up, keep track of its waxing and waning through the months, and make notes here when you spot a full or crescent moon. You might also look out for moon-related phenomena such as partial eclipses and earthshine, when the light that falls onto the earth is reflected back up and illuminates the dark portion of the moon.

Partial lunar eclipse

Date:

Notes:

Earthshine

Date:

Notes:

Crescent moons

Date:

Position:

Notes:

Date:

Position:

Notes:

Full moons

Date: ....

Position: ....

Notes: ....

Date: ....

Position: ....

Notes: ....

Date: ....

Position: ....

Notes: ....

Date: ....

Position: ....

Notes: ....

Date: ....

Position: ....

Notes: ....

Date: ....

Position: ....

Notes: ....

SPOT THE BRIGHT PLANETS

The 'bright planets' are Venus, Jupiter, Mars and Saturn. They are often brighter than the brightest stars and so are easily spotted even when you are just gazing out of city windows at night. You will need to know what you are looking for, of course, so use a resource such as *The Almanac*. It provides monthly lists of the moments that the bright planets are 'in conjunction with' (which means 'near') each other or the moon, along with the part of the sky in which to look for them. Record your sightings here, sketch their positions in relation to each other, and make notes about brightness and colour.

The moon and Venus

Date:

Your location:

Notes:

Sketch:

The moon and Jupiter

Date:

Your location:

Notes:

Sketch:

The moon and Mars

Date:

Your location:

Notes:

Sketch:

The moon and Saturn

Date:

Your location:

Notes:

Sketch:

FOCUS ON ORION

Orion is one of the easiest constellations to find in the sky. The distinctive trio of stars forming Orion's belt makes it highly recognisable, and Orion contains some of the brightest stars in the sky. It is particularly worth seeking out because the region of the sky in which it lies contains some fascinating non-star objects which you can peek at through binoculars or a telescope.

Find Orion

Orion is visible all year round, though it's at its highest in the northern hemisphere sky on winter evenings. Note its brightest stars, and take a closer look at them if you can: the blue supergiant Rigel is the seventh-brightest star in the sky, and the red supergiant Betelgeuse is the twelfth.

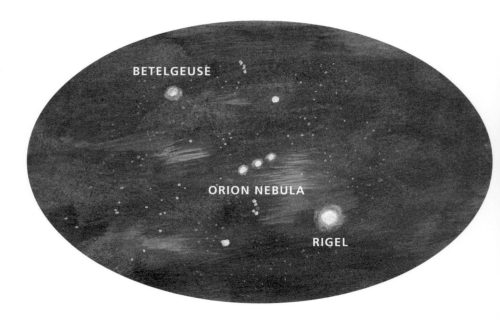

	Date:	Time:	Your location:
☐ **Orion**	....	....	....
☐ **Rigel**	....	....	....
☐ **Betelgeuse**	....	....	....

☐ **Find the Orion Nebula**

The Orion Nebula is a nursery where new stars are being formed. It is visible to the naked eye on a dark night, with its beauties really revealed through binoculars or a telescope. It is found below Orion's Belt, hanging like a sword.

☐ **Use Orion to find Sirius**

Sirius, the Dog Star, is the brightest star in the sky, and you can use Orion to locate it. Follow the line of Orion's belt, down and to the left, for about five times its length, and you will come to a bright and shining star: Sirius.

☐ **Use Orion to find Aldebaran and the Pleiades**

About the same distance in the other direction – up and to the right –you will find bright red Aldebaran, the brightest star in the constellation Taurus. Look about half as far again in the same direction and you will come across the beautiful Pleiades, or Seven Sisters, a cluster of seven bluish stars well worth looking at with binoculars or through a telescope.

STAR CHARTS AND CONSTELLATIONS

Over the next few pages you will find star charts for four months in the year – two charts for each season. Use these as a guide to finding constellations over the course of the year.

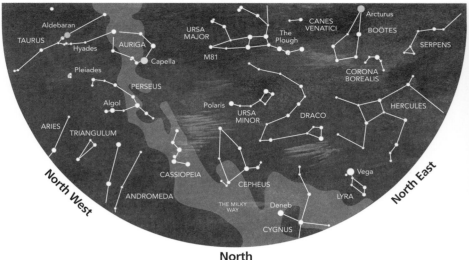

March – looking north at 10pm

☐   **Leo**   ☐   **Ursa Major, the Great Bear**

SPRING

The horizon is indicated by the curved edge of the chart. The chart opposite shows the view to the north, and the chart below the view to the south. Establish your compass points, then see if you can spot the constellations.

March – looking south at 10pm

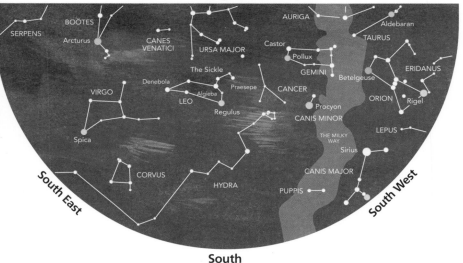

☐ **Virgo**   ☐ **Ursa Minor, the Little Bear**

SUMMER

The horizon is indicated by the curved edge of the chart. The chart below shows the view to the north, and the chart opposite the view to the south. Establish your compass points, then see if you can spot the constellations.

June – looking north at 11pm

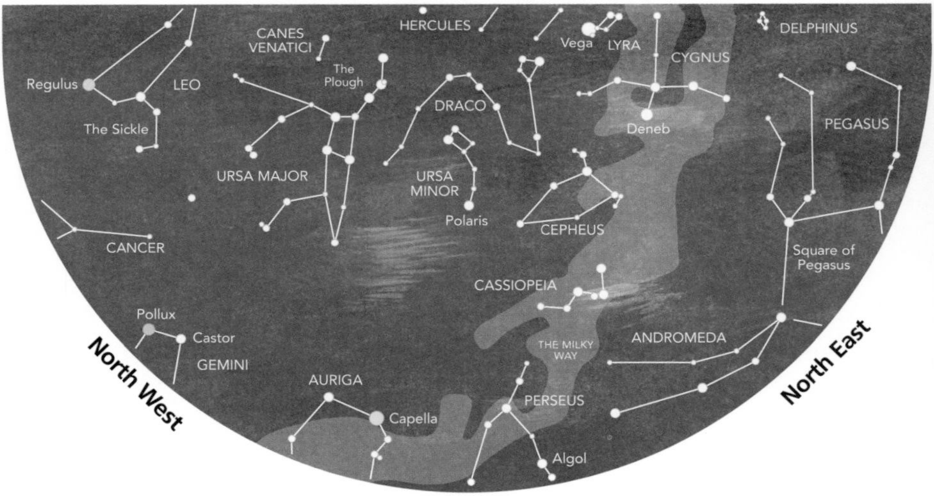

☐	**Cygnus, the Swan**
☐	**Boötes**

THE SKY AT NIGHT

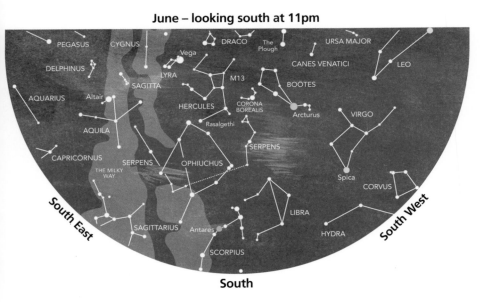

June – looking south at 11pm

Hercules

Draco

AUTUMN

The horizon is indicated by the curved edge of the chart. The chart below shows the view to the north, and the chart opposite the view to the south. Establish your compass points, then see if you can spot the constellations.

September – looking north at 11pm

OPHIUCHUS
LYRA
Vega
Deneb
ARIES
SERPENS
CYGNUS
TRIANGULUM
TAURUS
ANDROMEDA
Pleiades
CORONA BOREALIS
DRACO
Algol
HERCULES
CEPHEUS
CASSIOPEIA
Aldebaran
PERSEUS
Polaris
URSA MINOR
Capella
THE MILKY WAY
Arcturus
BOÖTES
The Plough
AURIGA
CANES VENATICI
North West
North East
URSA MAJOR

North

☐ **Andromeda**   ☐ **Pegasus**

September – looking south at 11pm

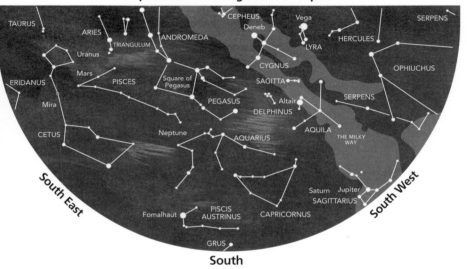

Cassiopeia   Cepheus

WINTER

The horizon is indicated by the curved edge of the chart. The chart below shows the view to the north, and the chart opposite the view to the south. Establish your compass points, then see if you can spot the constellations.

December – looking north at 10pm

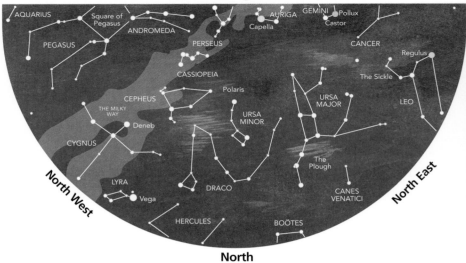

☐ **Gemini**   ☐ **Perseus**

December – looking south at 10pm

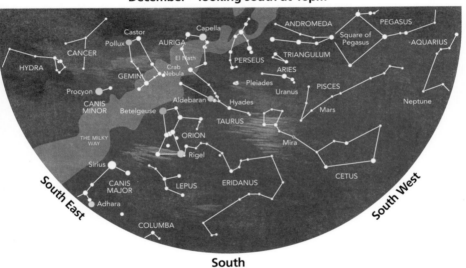

Orion ☐

Taurus ☐

South

THE GARDEN

MAP YOUR SPRING GARDEN

In spring, the most important thing to map is the whereabouts of spring bulbs, otherwise there is a risk of digging them up later in the season once their foliage has died down. Make notes here of any places that are bare in spring, so that you know where to plant more bulbs next autumn.

Highlights (What looks good this season?)

....

....

Plants to move (What don't you like?)

....

....

Plans for next season (What plants or features would you like but you don't yet have?)

....

....

Seasonal jobs checklist

Lawn:

....

Flowers:

....

Trees:

....

Structures and maintenance:

....

Wildlife patch:

....

MAP YOUR SUMMER GARDEN

As your plants come in to summer flower make notes here of flowering times and of particularly good combinations that you may want to repeat elsewhere. Are there any parts of your garden that could be improved with a few more flowering perennials?

Highlights (What looks good this season?)

....

....

Plants to move (What don't you like?)

....

....

Plans for next season (What plants or features would you like but you don't yet have?)

....

....

Seasonal jobs checklist

Lawn:

....

Flowers:

....

Trees:

....

Structures and maintenance:

....

Wildlife patch:

....

FLOWERS AND LEAVES –
SPRING AND SUMMER

Follow the instructions on page 33 for pressing flowers and leaves, then use a little glue to stick them onto these pages, creating a seasonal record of what is flowering in your garden in spring and summer.

MAP YOUR AUTUMN GARDEN

Even the smallest garden can be filled with autumn colour in the form of delicately hued perennial foliage and fiery shrubs. Map out what your garden does during this transition time: does it die back in a blaze of colour or just fade to brown? Where could planting improve that?

Highlights (What looks good this season?)

....

....

Plants to move (What don't you like?)

....

....

Plans for next season (What plants or features would you like but you don't yet have?)

....

....

Seasonal jobs checklist

Lawn:

....

Flowers:

....

Trees:

....

Structures and maintenance:

....

Wildlife patch:

....

MAP YOUR WINTER GARDEN

In winter you can see and map the bones of your garden. Do you need more evergreens for backbone? Would a splash of colour from winter bark be welcome anywhere? Consider also putting scented winter shrubs along paths or near windows, for a waft of spring-like scent on mild days.

Highlights (What looks good this season?)

....

....

Plants to move (What don't you like?)

....

....

Plans for next season (What plants or features would you like but you don't yet have?)

....

....

Seasonal jobs checklist

Lawn:

Flowers:

Trees:

Structures and maintenance:

Wildlife patch:

FLOWERS AND LEAVES – AUTUMN AND WINTER

Follow the instructions on page 33 for pressing flowers and leaves, then use a little glue to stick them onto these pages, creating a seasonal record of what is flowering in your garden in autumn and winter.

SEED ORDER

Use this space to write down the seeds you plan to order. You can do this ahead of the season, before ordering, or make notes throughout the season of your favourites and of recommendations from other gardeners, so that you are well prepared ahead of next season's ordering time.

Seed:	Supplier:	Date ordered:	Arrived:

Seed: Supplier: Date ordered: Arrived:

....

....

....

....

....

....

....

....

....

Notes:

....

....

....

....

....

....

....

....

....

....

....

MAP YOUR VEG PATCH

Use this grid to map your veg patch and to keep track of what you
are sowing where this year. This will come in handy next year as it is
always sensible to avoid growing the same annual crops in the same
place year after year.

Fruit/vegetable: Symbol

SOWING AND HARVESTING

Make a note of your sowing dates and varieties and then keep track
of how well they do by logging your harvest dates and yields.

Fruit/vegetable   Variety:
....

Date sown: Date first harvested:
....

Overall yield: Notes:
....

Fruit/vegetable   Variety:
....

Date sown: Date first harvested:
....

Overall yield: Notes:
....

Fruit/vegetable   Variety:
....

Date sown: Date first harvested:
....

Overall yield: Notes:
....

Fruit/vegetable   Variety:

Date sown: Date first harvested:

Overall yield: Notes:

Fruit/vegetable   Variety:

Date sown: Date first harvested:

Overall yield: Notes:

Fruit/vegetable   Variety:

Date sown: Date first harvested:

Overall yield: Notes:

Fruit/vegetable   Variety:

Date sown: Date first harvested:

Overall yield: Notes:

Fruit/vegetable

Variety:

Date sown:

Date first harvested:

Overall yield:

Notes:

Fruit/vegetable

Variety:

Date sown:

Date first harvested:

Overall yield:

Notes:

Fruit/vegetable

Variety:

Date sown:

Date first harvested:

Overall yield:

Notes:

Fruit/vegetable

Variety:

Date sown:

Date first harvested:

Overall yield:

Notes:

Fruit/vegetable

Variety:

Date sown:

Date first harvested:

Overall yield:

Notes:

Fruit/vegetable

Variety:

Date sown:

Date first harvested:

Overall yield:

Notes:

Fruit/vegetable

Variety:

Date sown:

Date first harvested:

Overall yield:

Notes:

Fruit/vegetable

Variety:

Date sown:

Date first harvested:

Overall yield:

Notes:

WALKS

WALKING RECORD

Keep a list here of the walks you take through the year. Remember, before you set out for a walk, you should always check that you have a map, a phone, water, snacks, plasters and suncream and a sunhat or a raincoat (depending on the weather). Always make sure you tell someone about your plans, route and timings.

Date: Location: Length: Time taken:

Pubs/cafés on route: Notes:

Date: Location: Length: Time taken:

Pubs/cafés on route: Notes:

Date: Location: Length: Time taken:

Pubs/cafés on route: Notes:

Date: Location: Length: Time taken:

....

Pubs/cafés on route: Notes:

....

....

....

Date: Location: Length: Time taken:

....

Pubs/cafés on route: Notes:

....

....

....

Date: Location: Length: Time taken:

....

Pubs/cafés on route: Notes:

....

....

....

Date: Location: Length: Time taken:

....

Pubs/cafés on route: Notes:

....

....

....

GEOCACHING

A worldwide treasure hunt that anyone can join at any time, geocaching is a brilliant way to enhance walks, particularly if you are dragging along reluctant children. A geocache is a waterproof container, hidden from view, containing a logbook for its finders to write in, and often a small selection of trinkets, too. It is tracked down using GPS coordinates and – when you get closer – your own nose for sniffing out treasure. There are millions of geocaches worldwide (there is even one on the International Space Station, should you happen to be up there), and there are almost certainly several within minutes of your front door.

Sign up for free at geocaching.com, then select a cache near you, put the coordinates into your smartphone and set off. Take a couple of little treasures along with you, to swap for something that someone else has left behind. Once you have found a geocache, write your name in its logbook and make your own log here.

Date: Cache name:

Description and hints:

Coordinates: Item removed: Item left:

Date: Cache name:

Description and hints:

Coordinates: Item removed: Item left:

Date: Cache name:

Description and hints:

Coordinates: Item removed: Item left:

Date: Cache name:

Description and hints:

Coordinates: Item removed: Item left:

Date: Cache name:

Description and hints:

Coordinates: Item removed: Item left:

Date: Cache name:

Description and hints:

Coordinates: Item removed: Item left:

SPOTTER'S GUIDE – WALKS

☐ **A cow**
Date: .... Notes: ....
....
....
....

☐ **A sheep**
Date: .... Notes: ....
....
....
....

☐ **A fallen tree**
Date: .... Notes: ....
....
....
....

☐ **Moss**
Date: .... Notes: ....
....
....
....

☐ **Lichen**

Date: .... Notes: ....

....

....

....

☐ **Animal tracks**

Date: .... Notes: ....

....

....

....

☐ **A kite**

Date: .... Notes: ....

....

....

....

☐ **A squirrel**

Date: .... Notes: ....

....

....

....

☐ **A river**

Date: .... Notes: ....

....

....

....

HOW TO MAP YOUR WALKS

The following pages provide space to create maps of some of your walks.
They might be big, day-long walks or little jaunts around your local
area: as long as you see something worth recording, the walks are worth
mapping. The point of creating your own maps is not to make proper,
to-scale, orienteering-standard maps, but to produce creative, personal
and beautiful mementos of your time spent walking. These will jog your
memory should you want to do the same walk again, or will simply be
enjoyable to look back on. You could just make a rough sketch or get out
the colouring pencils and create a thing of beauty.

1 Create your own legend for the map. What features did you see and
   which are you likely to want to include? You might want to make use
   of the symbols opposite or you might prefer to make up your own.
   As well as bridges, viewpoints and level crossings, you could mark in
   a magnolia that's in spectacular flower, a sea of bluebells or the spot
   where you saw a butterfly.
2 Sketch out your route, referring to a map for this or doing it from
   memory. Accuracy is not essential. Draw in nearby roads and railway
   lines and other major features that will help you orient.
3 Create a scale – this is possibly tricky and certainly optional, but even
   a rough idea will be useful to look back on.
4 Orient your map using the compass space provided.
5 Mark in the principal features of the walk using the symbols from your
   legend.
6 Fill in areas of housing, woodland and meadow, and then colour in
   everything to complete your map.

Footpath	– – – – –	Place of worship	
Cycle trail	· · · — · ·	Picnic site	
Road	———	Pub	PH
Bridge	)(	Café	
Railway	+++++++	Sea	
Woodland		Sand	
Stile		Cliff	
Hedgerow		Shore	
Meadow		Viewpoint	

MAP YOUR WALK

Location:

Date:

Weather:

Walk distance:

Walk duration: Walkers:

Points of interest:

WALK FINDS

Use these pages to stick finds from your walks, such as feathers, lichen and pressed flowers, to make sketches of the scenery or to attach photographs.

MAP YOUR WALK

Location:

Date:

Weather:

Walk distance:

Walk duration: Walkers:

....

Points of interest:

....

....

WALK FINDS

Use these pages to stick finds from your walks, such as feathers, lichen and pressed flowers, to make sketches of the scenery or to attach photographs.

MAP YOUR WALK

Location:

Date:

Weather:

Walk distance:

Walk duration:

Walkers:

Points of interest:

WALK FINDS

Use these pages to stick finds from your walks, such as feathers, lichen and pressed flowers, to make sketches of the scenery or to attach photographs.

MAP YOUR WALK

Location:

Date:

Weather:

Walk distance:

Walk duration: Walkers:

....

Points of interest:

....

....

WALK FINDS

Use these pages to stick finds from your walks, such as feathers, lichen and pressed flowers, to make sketches of the scenery or to attach photographs.

FOOD

FESTIVE AND SEASONAL FOODS

Keep a list of the festive and seasonal foods you cook throughout the year. There is space for your recipes on pages 115–117.

☐ **Forced rhubarb**

Date: .... Notes: ....

☐ **Seville oranges**

Date: .... Notes: ....

☐ **Wassail (hot mulled cider) for wassailing**

Date: .... Notes: ....

☐ **Pancakes for Shrove Tuesday**

Date: .... Notes: ....

☐ **Moon cakes for Chinese New Year**

Date: .... Notes: ....

☐ **Welsh cakes for St David's Day**

Date: .... Notes: ....

☐ **Chocolate Guinness cake for St Patrick's Day**

Date: .... Notes: ....

☐ **Hot cross buns**

Date: .... Notes: ....

☐ **Easter eggs**

Date: .... Notes: ....

☐ **Spring lamb**

Date: .... Notes: ....

☐ **Asparagus**

Date: .... Notes: ....

☐ **Atayef during Ramadan**

Date: .... Notes: ....

☐ **Ma'amoul for Eid**

Date: .... Notes: ....

☐ **Gooseberries**

Date: .... Notes: ....

☐ **Broad beans**

Date: .... Notes: ....

☐ **Fresh peas**

Date: .... Notes: ....

☐ **Fresh mackerel**

Date: .... Notes: ....

☐ **Brown crab**

Date: .... Notes: ....

☐ **Strawberries**

Date: .... Notes: ....

☐ **Cheesecake for Shavuot**

Date: .... Notes: ....

☐ **Cherries**

Date: .... Notes: ....

☐ **Crumble**

Date: .... Notes: ....

☐ **Quince**

Date: .... Notes: ....

☐ **Mont d'Or**

Date: .... Notes: ....

☐ **Toffee apples**

Date: .... Notes: ....

☐ **Diwali sweets**

Date: Notes:

☐ **Beaujolais nouveau**

Date: Notes:

☐ **Truffles**

Date: Notes:

☐ **Pheasant**

Date: Notes:

☐ **Sloe gin**

Date: Notes:

☐ **Bimuelos for Hanukkah**

Date: Notes:

☐ **Mince pies**

Date: Notes:

☐ **Christmas pudding**

Date: Notes:

FORAGING DIARY

Make notes of where and when you find the following so that you can go back to the same spot next year.

☐ **Wood sorrel**

Date: _____ Location: _____

Notes: _____

_____

_____

☐ **Wild garlic**

Date: _____ Location: _____

Notes: _____

_____

_____

☐ **Elderflowers**

Date: _____ Location: _____

Notes: _____

_____

_____

☐ **Nettles**

Date: _____ Location: _____

Notes: _____

_____

_____

☐ **Sweet cicely**

Date: _____ Location: _____

Notes: _____

_____

☐ **Marsh samphire**

Date: .... Location: ....

Notes: ....

....

....

☐ **Mussels**

Date: .... Location: ....

Notes: ....

....

....

☐ **Rosehips**

Date: .... Location: ....

Notes: ....

....

....

☐ **Haws**

Date: .... Location: ....

Notes: ....

....

....

☐ **Mulberries**

Date: .... Location: ....

Notes: ....

....

Blackberries

Date: Location:

Notes:

Damsons

Date: Location:

Notes:

Cobnuts

Date: Location:

Notes:

Wet walnuts

Date: Location:

Notes:

Blueberries

Date: Location:

Notes:

Sloes

Date: .... Location: ....

Notes: ....

....

....

Chanterelles

Date: .... Location: ....

Notes: ....

....

....

Puffballs

Date: .... Location: ....

Notes: ....

....

....

Sweet chestnuts

Date: .... Location: ....

Notes: ....

....

....

Hazelnuts

Date: .... Location: ....

Notes: ....

....

RECIPE NOTES

RECIPE NOTES

RITUALS AND CELEBRATIONS

THINGS TO CELEBRATE
IN SPRING

Use this list to spark ideas for your own rituals and gatherings and to celebrate the spring.

Saints' days: Celebrate the saints' days of Wales, Ireland, Cornwall and England in spring – St David, St Patrick, St Piran and St George all have their days in spring. Welsh cake, Guinness, pasties and a full English, ahoy!

Shrove Tuesday: This is the last day before Lent and the day on which those fasting for Lent need to use up all of their eggs and milk, hence the tradition of making pancakes. It is acceptable if not compulsory to eat pancakes for breakfast, lunch and dinner.

The vernal equinox: The moment at which day and night are the same length, after which day wins out over night, is the point in the year when we really start to feel that spring is irresistible. You could mark the moment by taking a walk and looking for signs of spring.

Spring bulbs: Look out for the first spring bulbs poking their heads optimistically above the soil. Keep a record of their dates and locations on a garden map (see page 58) or the spotter's guide (page 128). If yours are lacking, visit a garden with a good display, and make plans for next year.

Ostara: Neopagans believe that Easter is a Christianised version of a far older celebration of spring, rebirth and fertility called Ostara. Create an altar with nests, eggs, green or yellow candles and pastel-coloured spring flowers, or cut a branch and hang blown and painted eggs from it.

Easter: A mishmash of Christian and pagan symbolism, at Easter Christians celebrate the death and resurrection of Christ and his ascent to heaven. Bunnies and eggs and signs of fertility abound.

Bluebell woods: Walk in a wood at bluebell time – it's one of the great spectacles of our natural year, and so brief. The exact timing of the peak varies with the weather but it is generally around the end of April/ beginning of May. Research your local woods ahead of time, then stand by.

Passover or Pesach: One of the major Jewish holidays, during which Jews commemorate and celebrate the Exodus from Egypt with the Passover Seder. This is a ritualised retelling of the tale using a text called the Haggadah, followed by a feast.

Clocks going forward: British Summer Time and Irish Standard Time begin, so the clocks go forward by one hour, meaning that dawn and dusk arrive an hour later and making summer feel almost within touching distance. Sit out and enjoy the suddenly longer evenings.

April Fools' Day: Also known as All Fools' Day, 1st April has been a day for practical jokes since at least the time of the ancient Romans and Celts. Remember that your pranks and hoaxes must be played before midday, or you become the April Fool yourself.

May Day: A day to celebrate the glorious and fertile end of spring. Look out for May fairs featuring such harbingers of summer as Jack-in-the-Green, the May Queen, maypoles and chimney sweeps.

Beltane: This is a Celtic festival of summer, fire and fertility and was a traditional time for weddings. The Beltane bonfire was thought to have magical properties to ward off disease. A Beltane altar should be green and colourful and might feature ribbons, candles and spring flowers.

Dawn chorus: The dawn chorus reaches its peak in May as birds call for mates and use their voices to defend their breeding territories. Wake up pre-dawn, open the window and crawl back into bed as it starts up. You will soon find yourself listening to a glorious racket.

Rogation Sunday or beating the bounds: On Rogation Sunday (the Sunday before Ascension Day) an entire parish would come out to follow the ancient custom of walking around the perimeter of the parish. They would hit the boundaries with a stick to literally define them in case of incursions from neighbouring parishes. As a modern interpretation, you could do something community-minded – or perhaps think about and shore up your own personal boundaries.

YOUR SPRING RITUALS

What are the things you like to do every spring? Are there any new rituals that you would like to add? For example, you could have an Easter egg hunt complete with clues, or set your alarm and catch the full glory of the dawn chorus. Take inspiration from pages 120–21 and write down your hopes and plans here, and then use this space to make planning notes or write about them afterwards. You could also jot down spring birthdays and anniversaries here.

Ritual: Date: Location:

Notes:

Ritual: Date: Location:

Notes:

Ritual: Date: Location:

Notes:

Ritual: Date: Location:

Notes:

Ritual: Date: Location:

Notes:

Ritual: Date: Location:

Notes:

Ritual: Date: Location:

Notes:

YOUR SPRING GATHERINGS

Gathering: ....

Guests: ....

....

....

....

Menu: ....

....

....

....

....

....

....

....

....

Timings: ....

....

....

....

Gathering: ....

Guests: ....

....

....

....

Menu: ....

....

....

....

....

....

....

....

....

....

Timings: ....

....

....

....

....

Gathering:

Guests:

Menu:

Timings:

SPRING DIARY

Use this page to reflect on the season and what it means to you.

SPOTTER'S GUIDE – SPRING BULBS

Look out for the bulbs springing into life in your garden and in local parks and woods, and tick them off when you spot them.

☐ **Daffodils**

Date: .... Location: ....

Notes: ....

☐ **Wood anemones**

Date: .... Location: ....

Notes: ....

☐ **Crocuses**

Date: .... Location: ....

Notes: ....

☐ **Scillas**

Date: .... Location: ....

Notes: ....

☐ **Fritillaries**

Date: .... Location: ....

Notes: ....

☐ **Bluebells**

Date: .... Location: ....

Notes: ....

☐ **Irises**

Date: .... Location: ....

Notes: ....

☐ **Tulips**

Date: .... Location: ....

Notes: ....

☐ **Hyacinth**

Date: .... Location: ....

Notes: ....

THINGS TO CELEBRATE IN SUMMER

Use this list to spark ideas for your own rituals and gatherings and celebrate the summer.

The summer solstice/midsummer: Celebrate the pinnacle of summer in all its bright and warm glory, but with a wary eye to the second half of the year and the descent towards midwinter. You might want to get up early to watch the sun coming up on the longest day.

A summer picnic: When summer is doing its glorious thing, it is easy to forget how fleeting it is and to miss the moment. Set off, sausage rolls and lemonade in hand, for somewhere that is briefly at its peak, such as a wildflower meadow or a field full of dandelion clocks.

Summer sports: Mark out the dates of the Wimbledon finals and major football tournaments, buy in the Pimm's and the strawberries, or the beer and the crisps, invite a few friends around and settle in for an afternoon of shouting at the telly.

Make a posy of wild flowers: Flowers are in abundance in early summer so pick a few for a jam jar posy, always making sure to leave plenty behind to scatter seeds later in the year. As summer wears on you might pick golden grasses and a few of the first berries for your vase.

Pick-your-own: These fruit farms are a brief and seasonal treat, and a way to gorge on summer berries while getting enough fruit to preserve for the rest of the year. Fill baskets with strawberries, then come home and make your own jam and ice cream.

Butterfly sightings: Keep a look out for butterflies in your garden and keep notes so that you can compare next year. You could also log your sightings with the Big Butterfly Count, which takes place every summer.

August bank holidays: We are blessed with two bank holidays in August so plan days out or barbecues to make the most of them. The last one always feels like a significant marker before the official start of autumn.

Pride events: Pride month falls in June, and around the country throughout June and July there are Pride events that are always inclusive and celebratory. Attend a parade and take pride in yourself, your loved ones and the LGBT+ community in general.

Sea-swimming: The sea will be almost painfully cold at first, even at the height of summer, but if you can do it every day, or even every few days, you will soon become acclimatised. You may even continue swimming into the colder months.

Celtic harvest: Lammas is the old Celtic celebration of the first wheat harvest. A Lammas altar might involve a big pile of home-grown produce; candles in gold, yellow and orange; and a loaf of home-baked bread. A corn dolly wouldn't go amiss.

Notting Hill Carnival: This London event falls in late summer, a time to celebrate and appreciate Britain's African–Caribbean heritage. There are other summer carnivals in cities with large African–Caribbean communities around the country, so look out for them.

YOUR SUMMER RITUALS

What are the things you like to do every summer? Are there any new rituals that you would like to add? Perhaps you'd like to wake up early to see in the longest day, or have a picnic in a rose garden. Take inspiration from pages 130–31 and write down your hopes and plans here, then use this space to make planning notes or write about them afterwards. You could also jot down summer birthdays and anniversaries here.

Ritual: Date: Location:

Notes:

Ritual: Date: Location:

Notes:

Ritual: Date: Location:

Notes:

Ritual: Date: Location:

Notes:

Ritual: Date: Location:

Notes:

Ritual: Date: Location:

Notes:

Ritual: Date: Location:

Notes:

YOUR SUMMER GATHERINGS

Gathering:

....

Guests:

....

....

....

....

Menu:

....

....

....

....

....

....

....

....

....

Timings:

....

....

....

....

Gathering:

Guests:

Menu:

Timings:

Gathering:

....

Guests:

....

....

....

....

Menu:

....

....

....

....

....

....

....

....

....

....

....

....

Timings:

....

....

....

....

....

SUMMER DIARY

Use these pages to reflect on the season and what it means to you.

SPOTTER'S GUIDE – SUMMER BUTTERFLIES

Look out for these dainty beauties in summer gardens and parks, and tick them off when you have spotted them.

☐ **Common blue**

Date: .... Location: ....

Notes: ....

☐ **Gatekeeper**

Date: .... Location: ....

Notes: ....

☐ **Orange tip**

Date: .... Location: ....

Notes: ....

☐ **Red admiral**

Date: .... Location: ....

Notes: ....

☐ **Comma**

Date: .... Location: ....

Notes: ....

☐ **Peacock**

Date: .... Location: ....

Notes: ....

☐ **Small tortoiseshell**

Date: .... Location: ....

Notes: ....

☐ **Painted lady**

Date: .... Location: ....

Notes: ....

☐ **Swallowtail**

Date: .... Location: ....

Notes: ....

THINGS TO CELEBRATE IN AUTUMN

Use this list to spark ideas for your own rituals and gatherings and to celebrate the autumn.

The autumnal equinox: This is the moment when day and night are the same length; after this, night is in the ascendant. Now is the time to prepare for winter, practically and mentally: buy new winter boots, gather in logs and books and start on your vitamin D drops.

Mabon: The neopagan 'second harvest' festival, Mabon is a celebration of apples and other orchard fruits, and the spoils of the veg patch. Cook a hearty home-grown meal for friends, or make a Mabon altar rich in oranges, reds and yellows and spilling over with produce.

Michaelmas: This was once the end and the start of the administrative year, as harvests were tallied and new plans made. It was traditional to eat a goose at Michaelmas, fattened up on the stubble of the recently harvested fields, a tradition that is undergoing a bit of a revival.

Autumn leaves: Walk in a wood as the leaves start to turn, or visit an arboretum (a botanical tree garden) for really spectacular colours. This is one of those fleeting moments that are easy to miss, particularly if an autumn storm kicks up. Take some of the fallen leaves home to press (see page 33).

Back to study: New school and university terms start in autumn, and this is a time for fresh white shirts, sharpened pencils and polished shoes. Put aside the hazy, lazy, chaotic days of summer and look sharp: there's work to be done.

Rosh Hashanah: The start of the Jewish New Year, this is also a judgement day, when God weighs a person's good and bad deeds over the past year, to be sealed into the Book of Life on Yom Kippur. It is a time for taking stock and for introspection and repentance.

Clocks going back: British Summer Time and Irish Standard Time end, and nights are suddenly darker. This can be a bleak time of the year and a challenge for those trying to enjoy each moment. Embrace it with cosiness: soft blankets, lit fires, candles and box sets.

Hallowe'en: 31st October comes and it is time to dress up, get spooky and tramp around the neighbourhood knocking on doors and eating a bucketload of sweets. Or stock up, put out your pumpkin, decorate your house and wait for the terrifying seven-year-olds to come knocking.

Samhain: Closely related to Hallowe'en, this Celtic festival may have been its precursor. It was a time for divination and remembrance, when the veil between the living and the dead was believed to be at its thinnest. A Samhain altar might include apples, for divination, pumpkins and orange candles.

Bonfire Night/Guy Fawkes Night: This is the night we celebrate something nearly getting blown up by blowing up lots of small things. Bonfires and fireworks are obviously the main attraction, but you might also celebrate with toffee apples, parkin and spiced hot chocolate.

Martinmas: Traditionally marking the slaughter of farm animals for preserving over winter, this was also the occasion for tasting the first wine of the year. St Martin is the patron saint of beggars, and Martinmas is a time for hearty, meaty, wine-fuelled feasting, and for sharing with those less fortunate than yourself.

YOUR AUTUMN RITUALS

What are the things you like to do every autumn? Are there any new rituals that you would like to add? You might consider holding a harvest gathering with friends to show off your garden produce, or lighting a candle at Samhain to remember loved ones. Take inspiration from pages 140–41 and write down your hopes and plans here, and then use this space to make planning notes or write about them afterwards. You could also jot down autumn birthdays and anniversaries here.

Ritual: Date: Location:

Notes:

Ritual: Date: Location:

Notes:

Ritual: Date: Location:

Notes:

Ritual: Date: Location:

Notes:

Ritual: Date: Location:

Notes:

Ritual: Date: Location:

Notes:

Ritual: Date: Location:

Notes:

YOUR AUTUMN GATHERINGS

Gathering:

Guests:

Menu:

Timings:

Gathering:

Guests:

Menu:

Timings:

Gathering:

Guests:

Menu:

Timings:

AUTUMN DIARY

Use these pages to reflect on the season and what it means to you.

SPOTTER'S GUIDE – AUTUMN LEAVES

Look out for these leaves in parks, gardens, streets and woodland, and tick them off when you spot them.

☐ **Ginkgo**

Date: .... Location: ....

Notes: ....

☐ **Beech**

Date: .... Location: ....

Notes: ....

☐ **Oak**

Date: .... Location: ....

Notes: ....

☐ **Japanese maple**

Date: .... Location: ....

Notes: ....

☐ **Cherry**

Date: .... Location: ....

Notes: ....

☐ **Katsura**

Date: .... Location: ....

Notes: ....

☐ **Rowan**

Date: .... Location: ....

Notes: ....

☐ **Liquidambar**

Date: .... Location: ....

Notes: ....

☐ **Birch**

Date: .... Location: ....

Notes: ....

THINGS TO CELEBRATE IN WINTER

Use this list to spark ideas for your own rituals and gatherings and to celebrate the winter.

Diwali: This festival of lights, celebrated by Hindus, Jains, Sikhs and some Buddhists, symbolises a triumph of light over darkness and good over evil. Houses are lit with candles and lanterns, and sweets are shared.

Hanukkah: The Jewish festival of lights, Hanukkah commemorates a miraculous event involving a last flask of kosher oil lasting for eight days instead of one. Today, candles (in particular the nine branches of the candelabrum known as a menorah) or oil lamps are lit to commemorate the miracle, and fried foods such as latkes (potato pancakes) are eaten.

Midwinter/yule/winter solstice: It may be the darkest moment in the year but it's also a time for great hope and celebration, as the sun will soon spend more and more time in our skies. Mark it with a yule log and a toast to the coming warmth and light.

Christmas: This is the big one for Christians and for a great many others, too. Gather, eat, drink and exchange gifts, and reach out to those you haven't seen for a while, to show them you are thinking of them. Celebrate the birth of Christ and the coming of Santa Claus.

New Year's Eve: See in the New Year with a spectacular firework display, a lavish dinner party or just a book by the fire. However you mark it, this is a significant moment in the year for saying goodbye to the past and looking forward to the future.

Twelfth Night/Epiphany Eve: Falling on the evening of 5th January, this is the official end of the Christmas period, and the time to take down your Christmas decorations. Epiphany parties historically involved a cake with a bean and sometimes also a dried pea placed in the mix. Whoever found the bean would be crowned King of the Bean for the night, and the finder of a pea would be Queen of the Pea.

Plough Monday: The traditional start of the English agricultural year, this is when the ploughmen began work. Time to dig your soil and start planning for the growing year, or at least to order the year's seeds over a cup of tea.

Feeding the birds: Keep birds supplied with unfrozen water and high-fat foods to help them stay warm on long, cold nights. Take notes on visiting birds, or you could take part in the RSPB's Big Garden Birdwatch.

Wassailing: It is traditional on Twelfth Night to bless your apple trees to ensure a good harvest in the year ahead. Drink mulled cider (wassail) and tip a little onto the roots of a tree. A piece of toast soaked in wassail is left in the boughs as an offering to the tree's spirit.

Snow pleasures: When snow falls, get out as quickly as you can, as it often doesn't last. Pull on wellies and step out into the alien landscape, then head back inside for hot chocolate, knowing you haven't missed a thing.

Candlemas: Celebrating Jesus as 'the light of the world', Candlemas represents purity, hope and light. Candlelit processions are held and churchgoers bring candles into church to be blessed. It used to be believed that Candlemas was the only day when it was not unlucky to bring snowdrops into your house.

Imbolc: This is a pagan celebration of the beginning of the end of winter. Sow seeds, light candles and think ahead to spring. An Imbolc altar might include white and green candles, goat's milk or cheese, and a clump of snowdrops (provided you aren't superstitious – see Candlemas, above).

Chinese New Year: Celebrate the beginning of the Chinese New Year, which is based on the Chinese lunar calendar. It's a day that will bring luck for the year ahead for those who eat, wear and do the right things. Clean your house to make way for incoming luck, and wear red.

St Valentine's Day: It may be a hangover from the Roman festival of Lupercalia, in which young people of marriageable age drew lots for each other. Now we surprise the ones we love with a bunch of flowers or an anonymous card containing a rhyme or message.

YOUR WINTER RITUALS

What are the things you like to do every winter? Are there any new rituals that you would like to add? Fill your windows with lanterns at Diwali and share sweets with neighbours, or burn a special log and crack open the year's sloe gin at midwinter. Take inspiration from pages 150–51 and write down your hopes and plans here, and then use this space to make planning notes or write about them afterwards. You could also jot down winter birthdays and anniversaries here.

Ritual: Date: Location:

Notes:

Ritual: Date: Location:

Notes:

Ritual: Date: Location:

Notes:

Ritual: Date: Location:

Notes:

Ritual: Date: Location:

Notes:

Ritual: Date: Location:

Notes:

Ritual: Date: Location:

Notes:

GATHERINGS

Gathering: ....

Guests: ....

....

....

....

Menu: ....

....

....

....

....

....

....

....

Timings: ....

....

....

....

Gathering:

Guests:

Menu:

Timings:

Gathering:
....

Guests:
....
....
....
....

Menu:
....
....
....
....
....
....
....
....
....
....

Timings:
....
....
....
....
....

WINTER DIARY

Use these pages to reflect on the season and what it means to you.

SPOTTER'S GUIDE – WINTER BIRDS

The roster of birds you might see from your window has changed – summer migrants have left for the south and winter migrants have arrived from Scandinavia, Russia and mainland Europe. Country birds also come into the city during cold snaps. Look out for them along with our year-round residents, and tick them off when you see them.

☐ **Robin**

Date: .... Location: ....

Notes: ....

☐ **Fieldfare**

Date: .... Location: ....

Notes: ....